Etiquette at Table

The Classic Guide

This book is dedicated to Antoine, Anne Marie, Françoise,
Guillaume, and to the living memory of Ana and Théophile

The traditions and the correct techniques to eat at table are sociocultural codes that have evolved over centuries. Different societies have different codes; however, they all progressed to make meals a pleasant moment.

Etiquette is based on rational principles and pursues objectives always present in every social event. Know the rules of etiquette reduces the natural tension that arises from eating in public, decreases the possibility that something goes wrong and conveys credibility, for example, when you are having lunch with a potential client, business partner or employer. Often, meals are moments to define business strategies and agreements between individuals and so it can be very useful to find yourself in an advantageous position by having a full domain over the etiquette rules.

Regardless of our will, people might do comments about our character based on our behaviour at table. It is therefore important that all our actions reflect our true personality, avoiding unnecessary misunderstandings that may be difficult to change.

Often, the excessive concern about doing the right things makes us lose naturalness, precisely the opposite of what we intended to do. In this book we present suggestions that are very easy to learn, memorize and use, in order to eat with an elegant posture and without mistakes.

This book answers to pertinent questions that often arise from an invitation to dinner, where you can meet strangers. However, the information is suitable for other meals, including those you eat alone or with family and friends.

If the distribution and the variety of plates and silverware do not follow the suggestions stated in this book, you should accept it and refrain from making any remarks.

The suggestions written in this book are for right-handed people, left-handed should make the necessary adjustments when preparing for use the glasses and silverware. If you are left-handed, you should not change the position that the silverware has on table; just pick it when you prepare yourself to use it.

This book includes one appendix that suggests procedures for eating specific foods.

(1) After receiving an invitation to dinner, you should confirm your presence by letter, email or phone. Usually, invitations are received two to four weeks in advance and they should never be issued over the telephone in order to avoid engaging a person that do not wish to be engaged.

(2) If you are unable to attend, inform the hosts as soon as possible, and send a gift of recognition, such as flowers, wine, chocolates or any other nice gift.

(3) Write down in your agenda, the day and the hour of the dinner.

(4) The invitation may indicate the dress code; if this information is missing, you may contact the hosts. Take this opportunity to clarify any issue regarding food restrictions, although this matter is usually asked by the hosts.

(5) Plan what you will wear in advance because an excellent presentation is a sign of respect.

(6) Plan your route to the hosts' house in advance, and find out if there is any park for the cars or if it is better to go by taxi.

(7) If the dinner is informal, you may take wine, chocolates, sweets, books or any creative offer, but if the dinner is formal (state dinners, diplomatic receptions, etc.), do not take any gift. Avoid offer flowers, because

they require attention (put them in water, etc.) and the hosts may lack the time needed to do this.

(8) If necessary, take a light meal around two hours before the dinner, in order to avoid having too much appetite or overeating (this should always be avoided).

(9) Never take with you friends or family members (including descendants or ascendants) who were not invited

(10) On the day of the dinner, plan your schedule in order to arrive on time; any delay may be seen as disrespect.

(11) Do not arrive early; try to arrive exactly on time or up to five minutes later.

(12) If you are unable to attend, inform the hosts immediately. This should also be done if you are late.

(13) If you arrive too late and the dinner has already begun, do not greet other guests with handshakes, but bend the head slightly (we never use handshakes to greet someone who is already eating).

(14) Upon arrival, you can be greeted by a butler or any other house assistant who also receives your coat and all other accessories (umbrella, hat, gloves). In the absence of these, the coat and other accessories may be given to one of the hosts (only when he/she asks for them).

(15) If the hosts receive you at the door, greet them and be grateful for the invitation. If you bring any offer (casual dining), this is the right time to give it.

(16) The greeting is done by hand, firm without being too strong; kisses on the cheek are reserved for close friends (if the hostess offers you the face, you should give her two kisses, one kiss is only for very close friends).

(17) One kiss on the hand may be given to the hostess, but do not forget that one should not kiss the hand but only simulates. Do not make a bow; the hand of the lady should meet your lips and not the opposite.

(18) The hosts will take you to the room where all other guests are, and may suggest you a drink (always accept one, even if you do not intend to drink it). They will introduce you to other guests or to a specific group.

(19) You should not retain the hosts too long, but let them go, because they have other guests to attend.

(20) If the hosts cannot go with you to the room where all other guests are, you must go by yourself, select a drink from the table or among the ones that may be offered to you by the butler or any other house assistant.

(21) If the drink is too cold and the glass does not have a stem (if it has one, you should always hold it by the stem),

you can place a napkin between the glass and your hand in order to avoid the coldness of the drink.

(22) The glass should be hold with the left hand; the right hand must be free to greet other guests.

(23) When you are serving yourself with finger food (hors d'oeuvres), put only a few on your plate (maximum, three).

(24) In general, finger food is small enough to be eaten with one or two bites.

(25) If you are eating dried fruits (nuts, almonds, peanuts, etc.) place them on a small plate or on a paper napkin (right hand) and take them to the mouth (one at a time) with the left hand. So, if you have to greet someone with your right hand, it will always be clean.

(26) Do not introduce yourself to a group of people that does not know you; find out someone who already knows

you and may be willing to talk with you (never impose yourself to others).

(27) When you are in a group, avoid topics that exclude someone, for example, if he/she does not know subjects you are talking about, unless it is very relevant to all others.

(28) Try to maintain regular eye contact with everyone in the group.

(29) Do not start a private conversation with someone, excluding all others.

(30) When you are introduced to someone with great power or prestige, pay attention that although he/she may like the homage, sometimes he/she regard with contempt those who dispense it excessively. You should always act with respect, but simultaneously you should not forget the respect that is due to yourself.

(31) When possible, go to the toilette and wash your hands (at table, some food may be eaten with hands, without silverware).

(32) Once the meal is announced, place the glass on a table, and go ahead to the dining room.

(33) Do not rush, walk with serenity.

(34) Once you have arrived to the dining room, you may find a small board with the location of your table and your place (formal dinners with many guests). If there are few guests, it is possible that your name is written in front of the place where you should sit. Alternatively, wait for directions from the hosts (informal dinners).

(35) It is expected that the gentleman helps the lady who is at his right, to sit down.

(36) A gentleman does not sit before the ladies do so. He must wait until all ladies are seated, and never sits before

the hostess. It is also polite to wait for all older guests to be seated before he sits down.

(37) In order to sit down, you should move to the right of the chair, pull it out and sit to the left.

(38) After you are seated, place both feet on the floor, do not cross your legs (you may cross the legs at the ankles, under your chair) and do not stretch them.

(39) Never take your shoes off.

(40) The ladies may put the handbag under the table (a metal hook can be purchased in bags' shops) or, alternatively, and depending on the handbag size, place it on the floor (under the seat) or behind the backs (between the seat and back of the chair).

(41) Once seated, the gentleman should start the conversation with the lady who is at his right (do not look to any other guest nor to the table).

(42) Your body should not touch the chair back, except between courses.

(43) Talk alternately with the guest who is seated at your right and at your left. The general rule states that during the first course, the gentleman should talk with the lady who is at his right and during the second course with the lady who is at his left, and after adapts to the circumstances.

(44) Although it may be pleasant, it is impolite to monopolize the conversation with a lady or a gentleman who sits near you, preventing your interlocutor to devote part of her/his attention to any other guest.

(45) Do not ignore a guest who sits next to you just because her/his conversation is less interesting, this should serve as a stimulus to find subjects to talk about.

(46) When the guest of honour or the hostess withdraw the napkin from the table, you should also remove yours (at the restaurant, remove the napkin from the table soon after you sit down, do not wait for others to do it).

(47) Open the napkin over your lap; do not open it on the table.

(48) The napkin is placed on the lap; usually, it should be folded in half, with the folded edge closest to your body and the open side toward your knees.

(49) Do not adjust the napkin to the lap; just place it on the lap.

(50) If it is a paper napkin, place it on your lap as described above (do not leave it on the table).

(51) In some restaurants, it is the employee who places the napkin on your lap (sometimes, when the customer

leaves for a few moments and then returns, the employee brings a new napkin and repeats the process).

(52) The napkin is for wipe the corners of the mouth, the lips or the fingers. Wipe your fingers on the inside of the fold.

(53) If you must leave the table, place the napkin on your seat (it is not pleasant for other guests to see a used napkin on the table); if it is clean, you may place it at the left of the plate.

(54) The bread is broken with the fingers (never cut it with the knife); the butter's knife is used to spread the butter, not to cut the bread.

(55) If the butter is served in single portions, place small amounts directly on the bread, but if it is served in a butter's plate, put a small portion on your plate and then, in small amounts, on the bread.

(56) While you spread the butter, keep the bread on the plate, not on your hand.

(57) Spread the butter in a small piece of bread and eat it immediately.

(58) The bread goes to the mouth with the left hand.

(59) Do not use bread to eat the sauce that is on your plate, except when tasting olive oil; the bread is always eaten plain or with butter.

(60) Do not make any noise while eating.

(61) Do not drop food from your mouth.

(62) Eat with your mouth closed.

(63) The silverware that you first use is the one placed far from the plates. As the meal advances, you use the silverware progressively placed close to the plates.

(64) Do not touch the silverware that you did not use yet.

(65) While waiting for the food, keep your hands on your lap, over the napkin.

(66) Never clean the silverware that you will use (it is very offensive to the hosts); if you are in a restaurant, ask for another one.

(67) If you do not know how to use the silverware, see how the hosts behave and follow them (do not ask any question to any other guest).

(68) If you make a mistake when choosing the right silverware, continue eating with the wrong piece (do not put it back on the table).

(69) The food will be served on your left side (sometimes the soup may be served at your right).

(70) When the food or the wine is served by an employee, you may move away your body slightly, to the opposite side, in order to facilitate the service.

(71) If the dinner party includes few people (up to ten), you should wait until everyone is served before start eating (always after the hosts and the older guests).

(72) If there are many guests, you may start eating before the hosts, but wait until others have begun (avoid being the first), begin only after three or four guests have started to eat.

(73) If the hosts insist that you can begin your meal, and if other guests are already eating, you may start.

(74) When you start eating, do it gently, without rush, without noise.

(75) Never put too much food in your mouth.

(76) Swallow the food before you put more in your mouth.

(77) At lunch, the soup may be served in a bowl with wings. The soup is eaten with the aid of the wings or with a spoon (if there is any solid element in it). After you have finished, and if you used the spoon, do not forget to place on the plate, do not left it inside the bowl.

(78) At dinner, the soup is brought to the table in the soup plates.

(79) The spoon is held with the right hand, near the upper end of the handle.

(80) The spoon is held like a pencil; the handle rest on the middle finger and is held with the help of the thumb and the forefinger (the ring finger and little finger must be bent and near the palm).

(81) The spoon is filled with a smooth movement that takes it from the 6 to the 12 o'clock positions (imagine that the plate is a clock).

(82) Sometimes, a drop is formed at the base of the spoon. To avoid it, you may touch the underside of the spoon on the plate, near the 12 o'clock position (imagine that the plate is a clock).

(83) The spoon must touch the mouth by its side and not by its tip. This side position will prevent you to lift the arm excessively.

(84) The soup must be placed in the mouth without any noise.

(85) You should not forget that it is the food that meets the mouth and not the opposite.

(86) If you find a hair in the food, stop eating discretely.

(87) After you have finished, place the spoon with the handle near the 6 o'clock position and the tip of the spoon directed to the 12 o'clock position (imagine that the plate is a clock).

(88) Do not make any gestures while you have the spoon or any other silverware in your hand.

(89) Never talk excessively with the other guests that are near you; in general, people prefer to be heard and not to listen.

(90) If you do not know what to say, talk about cultural affairs (books, movies or theatre), travels and scientific issues.

(91) Never choose potentially embarrassing issues (never ask the age of your interlocutor) or issues that are not proper for the moment (illness or family problems). In the past, there were some taboo subjects like religion, politics, sport, sex, money or domestic employees, but

these can now be addressed in informal dinners, but not in formal ones. Remember that a dinner is not the most appropriate occasion to discuss potentially controversial issues.

(92) Never make confessions.

(93) Never make derogatory comments (especially about the dinner or the hosts).

(94) You must never depreciate yourself nor allow others to depreciate you.

(95) You must never do anything notorious that other guests may consider inappropriate.

(96) Do not ask questions that you wouldn't like to be asked about.

(97) When the employee offers you a platter, use the spoon and the fork that are placed on it and serve

yourself. Hold the fork with your left hand and spoon with your right hand. When serving yourself, keep the silverware as close as possible to the horizontal position.

(98) After serving yourself, place the fork and spoon together, at one end of the platter.

(99) If some food drops on the towel, pick up it with your own fork and place it on your plate (do not apologize, and behave as if this episode did not happen).

(100) Always be kind with the employee or any house assistant who serves you. After he/she serves you, you may look him/her and bend your head slightly. There is no need to talk, although you can offer occasional "thank you", but in a manner that will not encourage familiarity.

(101) Never lean over the table to reach something, just ask for it to one of the other guests.

(102) When you request something to a guest, do not forget to say please and thank you.

(103) If there is no employee to serve the meal, the platters are received and given by the guests, and should pass from left to right, in the opposite direction of the clockwise.

(104) Platters pass along the table and never across the table.

(105) Vegetables are placed in the plate, except the salads, which are placed on a side plate (other side plates are used only in restaurants, not at home).

(106) Serve yourself with small servings. If you like, you may serve yourself a second time, this is acceptable, but do not do it without being invited by the hosts.

(107) Never use your silverware to take food out of the platters, use the silverware that is on the platters.

(108) Never eat directly from the platters, the food must always be placed on your plate first.

(109) If there is a sauce intended to be served with the food, it is poured directly on the food and not on the plate.

(110) If you do not enjoy what you are being served, you can refuse it, but do not remain with an empty plate. Remember that this may be seen as a sign of disrespect. Under normal conditions, you should have informed the hosts about your food restrictions. The best option is accept small portions and left them on the plate, with discretion. If necessary, you can explain why you do not eat certain foods (allergy, temporary incapacity, religious issues, etc.) but do this only if one of the hosts asks you. Do not give any explanation to the other fellow guests.

(111) Fish is eaten with its own silverware (knife and fork).

(112) The fork is hold with the left hand and the knife in the right hand.

(113) The fork can also be hold with the right hand (in this case the knife remains on the table).

(114) The fork is hold with the tines facing down, when in the left hand, and with the tines facing up or down, when in the right hand.

(115) When the fork is in the left hand, its handle should touch the palm of the hand.

(116) The left forefinger is placed over the handle of the fork and this should be hold between the middle finger and thumb.

(117) The fish knife is used to separate the fish body and it is not necessary to use as much strength as in the case of the meat knife, so it is hold differently. The fingers hold

the fish knife in a way that the handle is placed between the thumb and forefinger (as if you are holding a pencil).

(118) To eat a fish that is presented whole, you should hold it firmly with the fork and, with the knife, open it by its side, from head to the caudal fin. Then, with the knife, lift the skin of the fish, midway, between the head and fin, gently pull it out, and place it aside. Start eating the fish near its head (the head should be on the left side of the plate). After eating the top area of the fish, lift the main fishbone, remove it, and eat the rest of the fish.

(119) If the fish does not have fish bones, it is perfectly acceptable to hold the fork with your right hand, and, in this case, the tines can be up or down, as it is more convenient to you.

(120) Taste the food before seasoning it (salt, pepper, olive oil, etc.).

(121) As a rule, you should not add salt or pepper to your food because this can be interpreted as if your hosts, or their chef, do not know how to seasoning it. If you are tempted to do this, put salt/pepper in the plate and not over the food. Then, when you are eating, touch the salt/pepper gently with your food.

(122) If the salt and the pepper cellars are both in the same set, they should not be separated. If someone asks you to pass the salt (or the pepper) cellar, you should pass them both, not only the salt (or the pepper).

(123) If a guest asks for salt, pepper, or any other item that is on the table near you, give it immediately and never use it while it is briefly on your hand.

(124) You can use the knife to press small portions of food some in order to help the fork to hold it. Instead of the knife, you can also use a small piece of bread.

(125) If you are eating with the fork only, do not forget to put it in the right hand, not in the left hand.

(126) When the fork is in the right hand, it can have the tines turned up. In this case, its handle rests on the middle finger with the support of the thumb and the forefinger (the ring finger and little finger must be bent and close to the palm).

(127) When you want to rest, put the fork in the plate with tines up or down (depending on how you are using it) with the handle near the 4 o'clock and tines towards 10 o'clock (imagine that the plate is a clock).

(128) Fish bones are removed from the mouth with the left hand fingers, not with the fork.

(129) When you are eating, keep the elbows close to your body, do not lift them unnecessarily.

(130) Do not talk with your mouth full, because you will not have a very good diction and also because something may drops from it.

(131) While using the silverware, look to the food and not to the guest who sits at your side or in front of you.

(132) When you are eating, position yourself in front of the plate, and remember that you should first put the food in your mouth and then turn to talk to the guest who sits near you.

(133) Place small portions of food in your mouth; this will avoid the situation when you have to swallow hastily to answer to any question. If you have small portions of food in your mouth, you can keep talking because this can easily be done.

(134) Do not put the elbows on the table, this golden rule can briefly be broken at the end of the meal, after all plates were removed (however, avoid doing this).

(135) You can rest your arms by putting the hands over the napkin or the wrists on the edge of the table.

(136) If you find something in the food that you do not want to eat, after it is already in the mouth, chew it into small pieces, remove it from the mouth with the fork and place it on the edge of the plate (you should not feel embarrassed, this is perfectly normal).

(137) In general, small pieces of food that cannot be swallowed, come out from the mouth with the aid of the same silverware (spoon or fork) with which there were placed in the mouth (there are exceptions, such as fish bones, which are removed by hand).

(138) After you have finished, place the knife and the fork together in a position close to the 5'o clock (imagine that the plate is a clock). The knife should have the cutting edge facing the fork and this should have the tines facing down and be placed on the left of the knife.

(139) The meat fork is used as the fork fish (with tines facing down), in the left hand.

(140) The meat knife is hold with the handle touching the palm, the forefinger extended over the handle (do not put the forefinger over the reverse side of the blade), and the thumb as side support, so that the pressure made by the forefinger is enough to cut the meat.

(141) When you are cutting the meat, the fork must hold the small portion that you will soon eat and the knife separates it from the rest of the meat. If necessary, you can press the meat with the knife while the tines of the fork penetrate it.

(142) Cut the meat that will soon eat; you should not cut several pieces at a time; this option prevents the meat to became too cool or too dry.

(143) The fork is brought to the mouth by a simultaneously rotation movement of the wrist and the forearm (you should not make any movement with the arm or with the elbow).

(144) As a general rule, the meat fork should always be in the left hand. Occasionally, if the meat dish has food that can be eaten with the fork only, you can place the knife on the plate and eat with the fork in your right hand. In this case, the knife should be placed over the plate with the handle positioned at two o'clock (imagine that the plate is a clock), the blade apex pointed to the twelve o'clock, and the blade facing the inside of the plate. Do not let the knife very close to the edge of the plate, because it may fall on the table.

(145) Never use a fork with the tines facing upwards (except when it is in the right hand, and, even in this case, not always).

(146) When you hold the fork in the left hand, never use it like a spoon, i.e., with tines facing up.

(147) If it is not necessary to use the knife to eat the meat dish, leave it on the table and use the fork in your right hand.

(148) Never use the knife in your left hand (except if you are left-handed).

(149) If you have already used the knife but no longer need it, place it on the plate in the resting position already mentioned.

(150) Never lift the knife more than two inches above the food that is on your plate.

(151) Never bring the knife to your mouth.

(152) When you are preparing to eat, you should bend your body slightly over the table, so that if some food falls, it will fall on your plate.

(153) If some food falls on your cloth, clean it with the napkin (if you are in a restaurant, you may request for a stain-repellent).

(154) Never transfer food from your plate to another guest's plate, nor receive it.

(155) Never crush food against the plate.

(156) Do not place all the food in the middle of the plate.

(157) If you want to rest, place the fork and the knife crossed on the plate (in the form of a circumflex); the knife with the handle between four and five o'clock (imagine that the plate is a clock) and the fork with the handle between seven and eight, both directed towards the centre of the plate. The fork should have the tines

facing down, be over the knife, and this should have the blade facing to the left (this is also a sign that the employee should not remove the plates).

(158) Do not place the silverware on the edge of the plate as if they are oars of a boat; once they have been removed from the contact with the table, they should never touch it again.

(159) After you have finished, you should place the knife and the fork together at a position close to 5 o'clock (imagine that the plate is a clock). The knife should have the blade facing to the fork and this should have the tines facing down and be placed left to the knife.

(160) After you have finished the meat dish, in which you used the fork only, put the fork in the 5 o'clock position, with the tines facing up.

(161) Salads are eaten as the meat dish, using the same etiquette rules.

(162) When the salad is served at the same time as the meat dish (in another plate), it is eaten with the same fork that you are using to eat the meat.

(163) When the salad is served after the meat dish (to clean the palate) it can be eaten with the fork and knife or just with the fork in the right hand.

(164) After the meat or salad dishes, all plates and side silverware that were not used, will be withdrawn from the table.

(165) The employee will then bring the dessert plates. Over them, a bowl with water may be placed, flanked by a fork (left) and a spoon (right). Often, the dessert silverware is already on the table, in front of you, near the plates (between the glasses and the place where the bread plate was).

(166) You must remove the bowl and place it in the place formerly occupied by the bread's plate (top left).

(167) Put the fork on the left of the dessert plate and the spoon on the right.

(168) The bowl with water is intended to wash the fingers, when you eat something without silverware. It may contain a piece of lemon, lime or petals of flowers (these elements must not be taken out) and it is used to wash your fingers tips for a few seconds (one hand at a time).

(169) Occasionally, the bowl with water may also be used at the beginning of the meal itself, if the main dish is intended to be eaten without silverware.

(170) Use the bowl of water to wash the tips of the fingers (not the hands).

(171) The fingers are dried with a brief touch on the napkin.

(172) The wet fingers can also touch the lips slightly, to clean them; these should be dried with the napkin.

(173) If the dessert is eaten with the fork in the left hand (tines down) and spoon in the right hand, it is the spoon that takes the food to the mouth, the fork only helps the spoon when you are preparing the food to be eaten.

(174) If the dessert is a cake or a pie, use the fork only (in the right hand) and leave the spoon on the table.

(175) If the dessert is ice cream or pudding, use the spoon only (in the right hand) and leave the fork on the table.

(176) The rest position of the dessert silverware is similar to the rest position of other silverware (fork with tines down, spoon with the concave part upwards, the tines of the fork over the spoon).

(177) Unlike the soup spoon (which just touches the lips), the dessert spoons can enter into the mouth through a slight rotation of the wrist. The spoon must approach the lips with an angle close to 45° degrees (90° degrees will be like a car entering in a garage and 0° degrees would be if only its side area touches the lips).

(178) After you have finished, place the spoon and fork together in the 5 o'clock position (imagine that the plate is a clock), the spoon with the concave part facing up, the fork with tines down, the fork on the left side of the spoon.

(179) If fruit is served, the employee will bring a plate with two silverware pieces (a knife and a fork); put the fork on the left side of the plate and the knife on the right side.

(180) The right procedures to eat fruit are described in the Appendix 1 of this book.

(181) Drinks are always served at your right side.

(182) When you decide to drink something, first swallow what you have in the mouth, then put the silverware in the rest position, wipe the lips, hold the glass by the stem (if it has one) and drink. If necessary, wipe the lips after drinking.

(183) The glasses are placed at your right, near the spoon and the knives.

(184) The glass of water is generally the largest one, followed by the glass of red wine and then the white wine glass; sometimes also exists a tall and thin glass for the sparkling wines.

(185) The glass of the red wine is wider than the white wine glass.

(186) The sparkling wine glass is higher, to prolong the release of the wine gas (carbon dioxide).

(187) Imagine the place where glasses are as being an imaginary clock: between 0 and 3 o'clock will be the glass of the sparkling wine, between 3 and 6 o'clock will be the glass of water, between 6 and 9 o'clock will be the glass of white wine, and between 9 and 12 o'clock will be the glass of red wine.

(188) You should not fill the glass up to its top (no more than half the capacity for the glass of red wine and two-thirds of the capacity for white wine).

(189) When the employee serves you wine, water or any other drink, let him do it with your glass on the table. If the hosts serve you, or if any other guest serves you, it is acceptable that in order to make their task easier, you take your glass to them, however, never tilt the glass when being served, keep it upright.

(190) If the water has ice cubes, take care not to put them in your mouth.

(191) Never add water to wine.

(192) Never drink excessively and never allow yourself to become drunk.

(193) Never serve yourself with water or wine without asking to the guests who sit near you if they want some.

(194) Do not hold any piece of silverware in one hand while holding the glass in the other hand.

(195) Never hold different kinds of food in your hands.

(196) If you spill a glass of water or wine over the table, put the glass in the upright position and continue as if nothing had happened (do not try to clean it with your napkin), the hosts will solve the problem.

(197) If you spill a glass of water on one of the guests, offer her/him your napkin, and tell her/him how sorry you

are (do not try to clean her/him because you might be misunderstood).

(198) If you break a glass, you can regret what has just happened (without excess); the hosts will solve the problem.

(199) You should never touch the glasses with your silverware.

(200) If someone makes a toast in his honour, you may raise your glass, but you should never drink its content.

(201) After you have finished your meal, do not touch the plates and do not push them away.

(202) Never ask the hosts about food that was not brought to the table nor given to the guests.

(203) Never talk about food that although being on your plate you do not intend to eat.

(204) If coffee or tea is served, do not leave the spoon in the cup, place it on the saucer.

(205) The hand that holds the tea or coffee cup should not have the little finger stretched, you should bend it like all other fingers.

(206) The fingers should hold the tea cup through the opposition of the thumb to the other four fingers, the fingers should not surround the wing.

(207) If any silverware falls on the floor, in a formal dinner, do not pick up it, use any other that is near you and continue as if nothing had happened. If it is an informal dinner, pick up it but do not use it.

(208) Do not sit back because this gesture can easily be interpreted as if you are uninterested in the conversation or in the meal.

(209) While at the table, do not touch your face nor your hair.

(210) Do not put the arm on the back of your chair.

(211) Never use toothpicks at the table (if you have food between your teeth, you should remove it in private).

(212) Do not yawn while you are at the table.

(213) Do not answer any phone call at the table (turn the phone off before sitting down; if you are expecting an important phone call, put your phone on the vibration tone, with no sound). If you forgot to turn the mobile phone off, and it rings at table, turn it off immediately, without even see who has called you, and apologize.

(214) Never raise your voice, because this can be interpreted as a sign of insecurity or disrespect.

(215) If none of the guests who sits beside you intends to talk with you, you may start a gently conversation with one of them.

(216) You should never feel intimidated.

(217) If the guest who sits next to you has some food between his/her teeth or in his/her clothes, you may tell him/her.

(218) If you have to blow up, turn around to the outside and do it with as little noise as possible (do not use, by mistake, the napkin).

(219) If you belch, apologize, and continue as if nothing had happened.

(220) If your stomach or intestines make some noises, ignore them and continue talking.

(221) Learn to control sneezing; if you have an attack of sneezing or hiccups, leave the room until they have gone.

(222) If you choke or need to cough, turn the body off the table and cover your mouth with a handkerchief or napkin. If necessary, go to the toilette. Return to the table, apologize and continue speaking or eating quietly.

(223) If you are choking and cannot breathe, ask help immediately (probably someone in the room knows how to perform the Heimlich manoeuvre).

(224) Never smoke at table.

(225) If there are no employees, you may ask the hosts if they want any help, but do not insist if you are told that it is not necessary.

(226) Do not apply cosmetics while you are at table.

(227) Do not consume pills or any other medicines in public, during a formal or informal dinner (get up and take them in the toilette), but if you decide to do it, be discrete and never place pills on the table.

(228) Never read at table (except when you are alone).

(229) Always be natural and stay comfortable.

(230) Never be surprised with the food that you are being served.

(231) If a new kind of food is served to you, something that you have never seen or tasted before, you should behave as if it is familiar to you, and do not make any comment about it.

(232) You should never finish the meal before the hosts, adjust your pace to them (ideally, everyone would eat with the same pace and finish simultaneously).

(233) At the end of the dinner, you may praise the food that was served to you, but without excesses.

(234) When the hostess finishes, the dinner is over.

(235) Do not get up while the hostess is still seated.

(236) Before you get up, put the napkin on the table, to the left of the plate, without bending it (never place the napkin on the plate). If there is no plate on the table, place your napkin where the plate was.

(237) Stand up, without noise, using the right side of the chair; if convenient, you may replace the chair next to the table.

(238) Do not to leave the dining room without the hosts do it first.

(239) If the hosts lead you to another room, you may sit wherever it is more appropriate.

(240) After 30 to 40 minutes, you may say goodbye to the hosts, to the guests and leave. If the group is small, you can say goodbye to the guests collectively, if it is a large group, you can leave without saying goodbye to them, but if you are a close friend to some guests, you should see them before leaving.

(241) Never leave without saying goodbye to the hosts.

(242) Express the intention to leave only once (do not state repeatedly that you must go, without doing it).

(243) At the door, the employee will give you your coat and other accessories (in the absence of an employee, the host/hostess may do it).

(244) When you arrive home, you may send an e-mail expressing your gratitude to the hosts; avoid calling, do this only if you are a very close friend.

(245) In the next day, you may send a gratitude letter, and also some flowers.

Appendix

Apple there are two options for eating an apple: (1) Hold it with your left hand, and, with the knife in your right hand, peel it into a very thin strip (1-2cm wide). This process should start at the top of the apple and, ideally, the peel should not break. Place the peel in the plate, cut the apple into quarters, remove the seeds and eat them without silverware. (2) Cut the apple into quarters, remove the seeds, peel up one of the quarters and eat it with your left hand. This procedure is then repeated for the other three parts.

Apricot peel it, cut it in two and eat them with your left hand or with a fork in your right hand.

Artichoke it is eaten with the hands. Take one bract at a time (right hand), put the basal part of the bract in the accompanying sauce, take it to the mouth and pass the more fleshy area on the teeth of the lower jaw, then place it back on the plate. When you are served the artichoke heart only, this is eaten with knife and fork.

Asparagus are eaten with your left hand (no silverware). If they are very long and thin, cut off the tip of it with the fork (right hand) and eat it with a fork. The basal part of the asparagus should be brought to the mouth with the left hand (no silverware). If the other guests use silverware to eat asparagus, do the same. If you have any doubt, always use the silverware.

Avocado if served in slices, eat it with the fork (right hand). If served in halves, hold one half with your left hand and use the spoon (in your right hand) to eat the edible mesocarp. When the avocado contains a salad (tuna, shrimp, etc.), hold it with your left hand and eat it with a fork, in your right hand.

Banana hold it with your left hand and peels it with the knife in your right hand. Place the banana peel on one side of the plate. Cut each end of the banana and place these two ends near the peel (do not eat them). Then, cut the banana into small slices and eat them with a fork.

Beer at table, drink the beer by the glass or by the mug (you may drink it by the bottle at a picnic or in a very informal occasion).

Blackberries are eaten with a spoon.

Boiled egg is placed in the egg holder with the sharp end facing down. Then, with the knife, break the shell along the perimeter of the egg, lift its top and eat the egg with a spoon.

Bread break small pieces with your hands and eat them with your left hand (bread is always eaten with the hands, never with silverware).

Candies are eaten one at a time. You should always eat the one you have touched. After touching it, do not put it back on the plate of the sweets. When eating sweets in a public place, put the wrappers in the trash, do not leave them on the table or in any visible place.

Caviar take a small portion and put it on your plate. Then eat it with small bread toasts (usually, caviar is placed on the toasts with a mother-of-pearl spoon).

Cheese must be cut with the care of leaving it with its initial shape. If the cheese is round, cut a triangular slice. If the cheese has the form of a large triangular slice, cut it along its length (do not bisect the tip of a triangular large cheese slice). If the triangle is small, you may eat the cheese beginning by the tip. Some cheeses have special procedures to be eaten, for example, some soft cheeses are eaten with a spoon, the Parmesan cheese is cut with a traditional knife, etc. The bread toasts that are eaten with cheese may be broken in small pieces; eat them with your left hand.

Cherries are eaten with the left hand, holding them by the stem; the pits are taken from the mouth with the aid of the index finger and the thumb (left hand). The pits should be placed on the plate, very close to each other.

Chicken is eaten with a knife and a fork (at a picnic it can be eaten without silverware).

Clams hold the clam shell with your left hand and take out the clam with a fork in your right hand.

Coffee never leave the spoon in the cup, it is placed on the saucer. Do not add iced water to cool the coffee nor dip cookies in it.

Corn cob is eaten without silverware; each hand holds one end of the cob. Eat a small portion only. If you want to rest, place the cob on the plate and wipe your hands in the napkin. Repeat this until you have eaten it all.

Éclair is eaten with the fork in the right hand.

Fig with the knife, you can cut it longitudinally, in four parts, and open it like the petals of a flower. Take one of the segments to your mouth (with both hands) and eat the fleshy part. The peels are placed on the edge of the plate, near each other. You can also eat the fig with a knife and a fork.

Gooseberries are eaten without silverware; to eat them, hold the stem of each one.

Grapes Cut a small portion with scissors and put it on our plate. Eat one grape at a time, without silverware, with your left hand. The seeds are removed from the mouth with the left thumb and forefinger and are placed on the plate, close to each other.

Hors d'oeuvre place them in your plate and eat them without silverware.

Ice cream eat the ice cream with a spoon; if the ice cream comes in a bowl with an accompanying plate, do not forget to place the spoon in the plate after you have finished.

Indian Food when food is eaten without silverware it is always eaten with the right hand, the left hand never touches the food.

Ketchup is removed from the saucer plate (or the vial) and placed in the plate. With the food in the fork, touch the ketchup slightly before eating it.

Kiwi is peeled with a knife, cut it crosswise into slices and eat them with the fork in the right hand.

Kumquat is eaten with its peel, with the left hand (no silverware); you may cut both ends with the knife before eat it. If they have seeds, these are taken from the mouth with the left thumb and left forefinger. Before you put the kumquat in your mouth, you can press it slightly to release the essential oils that are found in the peel in order to enhance its taste.

Lemon to apply some lemon drops to your food, press the lemon with your right hand and use your left hand as if it is an umbrella, in order to protect your clothes. Then put the lemon in your plate, near its edge.

Lettuce is eaten with the fork (right hand) and must not be cut. If the leaves are too large (this is not suppose to happen), you can use the knife (right hand) to support the fork (left hand) to bend them.

Lime to apply some lime drops to your food, press the lime with your right hand and use your left hand as if it is an umbrella, in order to protect your clothes. Then put the lime in your plate, near its edge.

Lobster use a combination of hands, silverware and other accessories. The body of the lobster is eaten with a knife and fork, or only with a fork. The clamps are eaten a special fork.

Loquat peel it with the knife, cut it in two halves and eat them with your left hand or with a fork (right hand).

Lychee is peeled with the fingers and eaten whole (left hand). The seeds are removed from the mouth with the aid of the left forefinger and the left thumb.

Mandarin peel it with your hands or with the knife and eat a segment at a time (left hand).

Mango is sectioned in two halves lengthwise (as if you are preparing fish fillets) and the seed is detached with the help of the knife. Then place each half of the fruit in the plate with their peel touching the plate. Hold one half with the fork and cut the edible parts in small squares with the knife. Bend the half of the fruit by its middle area, with your hands, in order that the squares became slightly detached. Eat them with a knife and a fork (or a spoon). This operation is repeated for the other half of the fruit.

Mayonnaise is removed from the saucer plate (or the vial) and placed in the plate. With the food in the fork, touch the mayonnaise slightly before eating it.

Melon if it is already sliced, it is eaten with a fork (right hand); if you have to slice it, eat it with a knife and a fork.

Mussel hold the shell with your left hand and eat the mussel with a fork in your right hand.

Nectarine cut it in two halves, remove the pit, peel one half with the knife, cut it in two and eat it without silverware (left hand) or with a knife and fork. Repeat this procedure for the other half.

Olives are eaten with the left thumb and forefinger, the pit is removed from the mouth with the same fingers. The pits are placed on the plate, close to each other. If the olives are included in a salad, they are eaten with a fork.

Omelette eat it with a fork in your right hand.

Orange there is three options to eat an orange. (1) Cut the peel, as you do with the apple, and eat the segments individually, without silverware (left hand). (2) Hold the orange with your left hand and cut the peel from top to bottom with the knife, without removing it. Then, with the knife, strip the peel lengthwise and place it on the plate. Remove the segments with the help of the knife and eat each segment at a time without silverware (left hand). (3) Peel it, cut it into transversal slices and eat them with a knife and a fork.

Oyster is eaten raw with a few drops of lemon. Hold it with your left hand and open the oyster shell with a special fork in your right hand (a common fork will also do). Place the oyster into your mouth and swallow it (do not chew it). You may also drink the liquid that remains in the oyster shell.

Papaya hold it with your left hand, cut it lengthwise, remove the seeds (with a spoon) and eat it with a spoon.

Pâté is spread over a small toast and eaten (left hand). While spreading the pâté, the toast remains on the plate, not on the hand.

Peach cut it in two halves, remove the pit, peel one half, cut it in two and eat them without silverware (left hand) or with a knife and a fork. Repeat this procedure for the other half.

Pear the procedure is similar to the apple. Alternatively, cut the pear into quarters, remove the seeds, peel them with a knife and eat them with a knife and a fork.

Peas never press them, with the fork, against the plate. If necessary, they are grouped against the tines of the fork with the aid of the knife blade.

Pie eat it with a fork in your right hand. Some pies (fruit, etc..) can also be eaten with a fork and a spoon, in this case the fork (left hand) holds the pie and the spoon (right hand) cuts it. The silverware that goes to the mouth is the spoon.

Pineapple cut a slice, peel it with a knife and eat it with a knife and a fork (do not eat the central area because it is very fibrous).

Pizza is eaten with a knife and a fork.

Plum peel it, cut it in two halves, remove the pit, and eat them with your left hand or with a fork.

Pomegranate is not peeled at table; the seeds are eaten with a spoon.

Pudding is eaten with a fork (left hand) and spoon (right hand); the fork helps the spoon. The silverware that goes to the mouth is the spoon. Alternatively, eat it with the spoon only (right hand).

Quail eggs are brought to the table whole. Break one at a time, peel it, touch it in the sauce and eat it whole (left hand).

Raspberries are eaten with a spoon.

Risotto is eaten with a spoon or fork (the right hand). Move the portion that you want to eat to the edge of the plate to cool it, and eat it. Repeat this procedure as often as necessary. If you do this, the rice that remains in the centre of the plate is kept warm.

Salt In formal dinners, salt is in an open salt cellar, placed on the table and you can use a salt spoon or your own fingers to place it in your plate. Place a small amount of salt in the plate and, before eating, touch it with the food in your fork.

Sandwich If it is very thin, it can be eaten with a knife and a fork. If it is large and has many items inside the bread, it should be eaten with both hands.

Shrimps if they are served as a main dish eat them with a knife and a fork. If they are in a creative dish and still have the tail, hold them by the tail and eat them. A cocktail shrimp is eaten with the fork (right hand).

Soufflé is eaten with the fork (right hand).

Spaghetti is eaten with a fork (right hand). The fork is placed vertically in the centre of the plate and it is rotated to the edge of it. Once it has reached the edge, the spaghetti is already wrapped in the tines of the fork. You can also use a spoon (left hand) to help wrap the spaghetti instead of doing it over the plate. Wrap only two or three strands of spaghetti at a time.

Strawberries if they are much sectioned, they are eaten with a spoon, otherwise hold them by the stem and eat them (left hand). The strawberry fork is used to pierce it and then dip it into a bowl of whipped cream, sour cream, or sugar.

Tangerines peel them with the hands or with the knife, and eat each segment at a time (left hand).

Tea milk, cream or lemon are added after the tea is in the cup, never before. Do not leave the spoon in the cup; place it on the saucer. Never add iced water to cool the tea, nor dip biscuits in it.

Tisane do not leave the spoon in the cup; always put it on the saucer. Never add iced water to cool a tisane, nor dip biscuits in it.

Water always drink it slowly; if it has ice cubes, do not place them in your mouth.

Watermelon eat small portions, with the fork in your right hand.

www.ingramcontent.com/pod-product-compliance
Lightning Source LLC
Chambersburg PA
CBHW071113280526
45787CB00003B/1020